SIMONE FILIPPONE

THE FUNDAMENTALS OF C: TIPS AND TRICKS

A TRUE DEVELOPER (ALMOST) ALWAYS STARTS FROM ZERO

Special thanks to Professor M.C. and Professor G.T., who made me love this subject

Summary

Introduction

A true developer always starts from number zero. The opening sentence of the book is true for all developers who are beginning to program or who are already experts in the field. A universal law in short! However, leaving those things aside, this guide will focus mainly on the software part and there are some "tricks" to make your program faster and more competitive. We will start with the basics and get down to vectors (arrays), the stack etc. Even before programming, it is necessary to introduce the concept of machine and machine language because the C language is very close to it. The computer "understands" only electrical signals, zero and one as input, and we through C and a compiler are able to translate the source code into machine language and the computer will execute it. To compile the code you need a compiler, such as visual studio code or a simple online compiler is fine (I personally recommend the onlinegbd compiler) . A typical program contains at least one library (necessary for the standard functions we are going to use), the main function (main), and many curly brackets. If you are just starting out, it will seem very difficult indeed to be able to program in this language, but don't give up! It only takes a few hours of practice and a lot of patience to start creating programs that work. Don't worry, with this guide, you will not only be able to start programming, but if you already know how to do it, it will help you "enhance" your code and use some tricks to speed up code execution. Another key side to consider is time. Time is critical in programming, because code that uses more time is generally worse than code that uses less time. This is especially true for those programs that contain nested loops (i.e., machine loops in other machine loops that execute instructions) and can potentially take up a lot of time and resources. This guide also contains exercises to practice, such as an empty program to complete to achieve a certain goal. We will start with the variables and the explanation of the first functions.

Variables

Variables are fundamental objects in general programming because they keep track of the data we accumulate from mathematical and non-mathematical operations, such as an addition or the result of a function. More easily, a variable is an empty container that can be filled with data, such as integers, floating numbers, booleans, etc. But let's start with the most common ones, the integers.

Integers can only contain natural numbers, such as positives and negatives. The limitation of this int variable is that it can store numbers ranging from -2147483648 up to 2147483647 (zero is included among the positive numbers). To assign a value to a variable you must use the = symbol and specify the type of the variable first.

An example: int a = 10. In this case we are going to assign the value 10 in the integer variable a, which will hold this value in memory until the variable is overwritten.

An example: int a = 10 a = 20. The value of a is overwritten to 20.

A program that runs something like this is written like this:

```c
#include <stdio.h>

int main()
{
    int a = 10;
    a = 20;
}
```

Now, however, if we go to compile the program absolutely nothing will happen because there is no function that goes to print the result of our operations.
The basic function that succeeds best for this purpose is the printf function: `printf("");`

For now, we will limit ourselves to knowing that the printf function is used to print the result of a function or data taken as input. This function will be covered later.
Note: You can name the variables any way you want.

```c
#include <stdio.h>

int main()
{
    int a = 10;
    a = 20;
    printf("%d", a);
}
```

This program will print the number 20 in the output, remember to always put semicolons and in the printf must be put %d, which indicates to print an integer value.

Output: `20`

If, on the other hand, we write a program like:

```c
#include <stdio.h>

int main()
{
    int a = 10;
    int b = 20;
    int c = 0;
    c = a + b;
    printf("the value of c is: %d", c);
}
```

The printf function will print the number 30, which would be the result of the addition between the variable a containing 10 and the variable b containing 20.

Output:
```
the value of c is: 30
```

Another possible operation is this:
```c
#include <stdio.h>

int main()
{
    int a = 10;
    int b = 5;
    b = b + a;
    printf("the value of b is: %d", b);
}
```

Output:
```
the value of b is: 15
```

In this case we create two variables and initialize them (a is 10 and b is 5) and then we go to update the value of b by doing the addition between a and b and writing the result into the variable b. The printf will print 15.

Now you may be wondering: what if, for example, I want to do operations over 2 billion numbers? In this case we need to use variables such as long int and long long int for operations that require us to store numbers well beyond 2 billion.

A variable of type long long int can range from -9 223 372 036 854 775 808 to +9 223 372 036 854 775 807. Not bad, is it?

If we need even more numbers we can create a variable of unsigned type, this however only works with positive numbers and we can go up to a maximum of +18 446 744 073 709 551 615.

The use of these variables is the same as the variable of type int, only some things vary such as the increased use of memory and we go from %d to %ld in the case of long int or %lld for long long int:

```c
#include <stdio.h>

int main()
{
    long int a = 10;
    printf("the value of a is: %ld\n", a);
    long long int b = 10;
    printf("the value of b is: %lld", b);

}
```

Output:

```
the value of a is: 10
the value of b is: 10
```

The program will print the value of the variables. If you try to assign a value that cannot be assigned to a variable, the value stored in the variable will probably be incorrect, since the compiler will warn you of an overflow problem. Put more simply, if you try to put 10 liters of water into a container that can only hold 5 liters, the excess water will flow out of the container.

Here is an example on how int and long long int **should not be used:**

```c
#include <stdio.h>

int main()
{
    int a = 1000000000000;
    printf("the values of a is: %d", a);
    long long b = 10;
    printf("the values of b is: %lld", b);

}
```

Variable a cannot hold that number since it is too large, while variable b is not really an error but is more a bad management of memory.

Char variables are used to store individual characters and actually, the computer reads them as integer values, since char ranges from -128 up to 127, although we will actually dwell on positive numbers. Each character corresponds to an **ASCII** (American Standard Code for Information Interchange) numeric code. For example: the number 0 is identified with the number 48, 1 with 49, 2 with 50 etc.

Here is an example for using the characters:

```c
#include <stdio.h>

int main()
{
    char a = 48;
    char b = 65;
    printf("the value of a is: %c\n", a);
    printf("the value of b is: %c", b);
}
```

Output:
```
the value of a is: 0
the value of b is: A
```

Here a version of the ASCII table, where Char stands for character and DEC stands for Decimal numerical system:

ASCII CODE Chart - Character and their equivalent decimal values

Char	NUL	SOH	STX	ETX	EOT	ENQ	ACK	BEL	BS	HT	LF	VT	FF	CR	SO	SI
DEC	00	01	02	03	04	05	06	07	08	09	10	11	12	13	14	15
Char	DLE	DC1	DC2	DC3	DC4	NAK	SYN	ETB	CAN	EM	SUB	ESC	FS	GS	RS	US
DEC	16	17	18	19	20	21	22	23	24	25	26	27	28	29	30	31
Char	SP	!		#	$	%	&	'	(	)	*	+	,	-	.	/
DEC	32	33	34	35	36	37	38	39	40	41	42	43	44	45	46	47
Char	0	1	2	3	4	5	6	7	8	9	:	;	<	=	>	?
DEC	48	49	50	51	52	53	54	55	56	57	58	59	60	61	62	63
Char	@	A	B	C	D	E	F	G	H	I	J	K	L	M	N	O
DEC	64	65	66	67	68	69	70	71	72	73	74	75	76	77	78	79
Char	P	Q	R	S	T	U	V	W	X	Y	Z	[	\	]	^	_
DEC	80	81	82	83	84	85	86	87	88	89	90	91	92	93	94	95
Char	`	a	b	c	d	e	f	g	h	i	j	k	l	m	n	o
DEC	96	97	98	99	100	101	102	103	104	105	106	107	108	109	110	111
Char	p	q	r	s	t	u	v	w	x	y	z	{			}	~	DEL
DEC	112	113	114	115	116	117	118	119	120	121	122	123	124	125	126	127

The \n character is useful for carriage return and thus prevents printfs from overlapping. In this case, in the variable a there is the number 48 representing zero and in the variable b there is the number 65 representing the letter A. Another thing to note is that you no longer need %d but %c to print characters.

Another important variable type to know about is floating point and double, which are useful for doing mathematical operations with all number (for example 8.2 * 8.2). The major difference between these two types is that floating point uses 4 bytes (32 bits) and double has twice the precision and uses 8 bytes (64 bits). For example:

```c
#include <stdio.h>

int main()
{
    float a = 0.0;
    printf("the values of a is: %f\n", a);
    float b = 0.1;
    printf("the values of b is: %f", b);

}
```

Output:
```
the values of a is: 0.000000
the values of b is: 0.100000
```

In this case, however, there is a small problem, namely, the digits represented after the decimal point are not 1 as we would like but are the standard 6 digits of the float and double types.
In fact, the program will print the value of a that is 0.000000 and b is 0.100000. If you want to avoid this, just add to %f (typical for printing floats) a %.1f, which means to print only one digit after the decimal point (if you want more just change the number after the point, if you want 2 for example you can do %.2f:

This will print 0.0 for **a** and 0.10 for **b**:

```c
#include <stdio.h>

int main()
{
    float a = 0.0;
    printf("the values of a is: %.1f\n", a);
    float b = 0.1;
    printf("the values of b is: %.2f", b);

}
```

Output:
```
the values of a is: 0.0
the values of b is: 0.10
```

```c
#include <stdio.h>

int main()
{
    float a = 0.0;
    printf("the values of a is: %.8f\n", a);
    float b = 0.1;
    printf("the values of b is: %.8f", b);

}
```

Output:
```
the values of a is: 0.00000000
the values of b is: 0.10000000
```

The standard C functions (printf and scanf)

These two standard C functions are very important, since they allow the user to input data from the keyboard and print them as output on the screen. To use them you must include (#include) the stdio.h library (which stands for standard input/output).

```c
#include <stdio.h>
```

As the name suggests, the printf function is used to print something on the computer monitor, such as the value of a variable or text typed by us:

```c
#include <stdio.h>

int main()
{
    int a = 10;
    printf("Hello World\n");
    printf("the value of a is: %d\n", a);
    printf("the modified value of a is: %d", a+20);

}
```

These three functions will print respectively:

```
Hello World
the value of a is: 10
the modified value of a is: 30
```

The scanf function, on the other hand, is used to take input from the user's keyboard. The data that can be taken are all those addressed so far and also other types. This is the right semantics for the scanf function to work:

```c
scanf("%d",&a);
```

The semantic is similar to the printf function, except that after the comma the & must be added and you cannot write inside scanf. Note well that this semantics applies only to integers. If you want long long int numbers instead then it is always necessary to replace the %d with %lld.

An example with the scanf:

```c
#include <stdio.h>
```

```c
int main()
{
    int a = 0;
    printf("insert a number\n");
    scanf("%d", &a);
    printf("the inserted number is: %d", a);

}
```

Output (the input was taken by the keyboard):

```
insert a number
0
the inserted number is: 0
```

In this example, I used printf and scanf together to let the user
know that the program requires a data entry and the program
will wait until the user enters data.
It is not necessary to use the first printf in the example, but it is
always recommended. If, on the other hand, you want to insert
characters, simply change %d to %c in the scanf function:

```c
#include <stdio.h>
int main()
{
    char a = ' ';
    printf("insert a character\n");
    scanf("%c", &a);
    printf("the inserted character is: %c", a);
```

Output (the input was taken by the keyboard):

```
insert a character
a
the inserted character is: a
```

Note that character type variables should be used with the ' ' and
not with " ".

Multiple scanf (or you can add a %d or whatever and & +
variable name) are needed to take more than one different
variable as input (this problem will be addressed later with loops,
since without them it would be very difficult to make programs
to store e.g. 900 different numbers).

This is an example:

```c
#include <stdio.h>

int main()
{
    int a = 0;
    int b = 0;
    printf("insert a number\n");
    scanf("%d", &a);
    printf("insert another number\n");
    scanf("%d", &b);
    printf("the inserted numbers are: %d %d", a, b);

}
```

Output (the input was taken by the keyboard):

```
insert a number
0
insert another number
1
the inserted numbers are: 0 1
```

If you do this is also correct:

```c
#include <stdio.h>

int main()
{
    int a = 0;
    int b = 0;
    printf("insert a number\n");
```

```c
    scanf("%d %d", &a, &b);
    printf("the inserted numbers are: %d %d", a, b);

}
```

If-Else and Switch Statements

These two statements are important to impose specific
conditions on the program. For now, we will dwell on the if
statement since to use the else statement, one must know the if
statement well first. As mentioned earlier, certain conditions
must be put in the if to make the program execute specific
blocks of instructions, including, for example, checking whether
a number is even or odd, or checking whether a number is
divisible by another number etc.
The semantics of the if is:

```c
#include <stdio.h>

int main()
{
    if(/*instruction1*/)
    {
        //execute the code if the instruction1 is true
    }
    //the code after the if will be executed next,
    //regardless of whether instruction1 is true or
false.
}
```

Note that the characters // and /* */ will be explained later, in
short they are expressions to comment on the code. In this case
we have only one if with only one condition to check (since
multiple conditions can be entered) and we have also inserted
curly brackets to make the entire block of instructions execute,
because without them only one instruction will be executed.

This is an example on the if:

```c
#include <stdio.h>

int main()
{
    int a = 10;
    if(a == 10) //the == statement is different from =
    {
        printf("the number a is 10");
    }
    if(a != 10) //the != statement stands for "different"
    {
        printf("the number is not 10");
    }
}
```

Output:

```
the number a is 10
```

With this code the condition in the if will be printed, since the variable a contains the number 10 and in the if the condition "if the variable a is equal to 10 (== statement)" is checked, then do these statements inside the curly brackets. Obviously the == statement is different from =, because == stands for "is equal to?" while the = statement stands for "assigns the value to a variable."

An example for checking whether an input number is positive or negative might be:

```c
#include <stdio.h>

int main()
{
    int a = 0;
    printf("insert a number: ");
    scanf("%d", &a);
```

```c
    if(a >= 0)
    {
        printf("the chosen number is positive\n");
    }


    if(a < 0) //we consider 0 as a positive number
    {
        printf("the chosen number is negative\n");
    }
}
```

Output (the input was taken by the keyboard):

```
insert a number: 0
the chosen number is positive
```

In this example if, for example, 0 is entered, the first if will be executed, since 0 is greater or equal to zero (>= statement), but if -100 is entered, the second if will be executed, since -100 is less than zero (a < 0 statement).
This code could also have been written with a simple if and an else, since the else serves as a contrary condition to the first if. An example to be clearer:

```c
#include <stdio.h>

int main()
{
    int a = 0;

    printf("insert a number: ");
    scanf("%d", &a);

    if(a >= 0)
    {
        printf("the chosen number is positive\n");
    }

    else
```

```c
    {
        printf("the chosen number is negative\n");
    }
}
```

If we want to create a program that checks if an input number is even or odd we can do it like this:

```c
#include <stdio.h>


int main()
{
    int a = 0;
    printf("insert a number: ");
    scanf("%d", &a);

    if(a % 2 == 0)
    {
        printf("the chosen number is even\n");
    }
    if(a % 2 != 0)
    {
        printf("the chosen number is odd\n");
    }
}
```

Output (the input was taken by the keyboard):

```
insert a number: 0
the chosen number is even
```

The % statement means that the division is done and returns the remainder, so if with division by 2 the result is zero, so no remainder, then it means the number is even, while if it gives remainder it means the number is odd. With the if statement (and loops or other statements) you can also use several logical operators to create even more elaborate conditions to make the code work better. The most common logical operators to use are && (AND), || (OR), ! (NOT).

This is an example:

```c
#include <stdio.h>
int main()
{
    int a = 10;
    int b = 20;
    int c = 30;
    if(a == 10 && b == 20)
    {
        printf("a is equal to 10 and b is equal to
20\n");
    }

    if(!a == 0)
    {
        printf("a is not 0\n");
    }

    if(a == 10 || b == 0 || c == 0)
    {
        printf("one variable is equal to the number set
in the if");
    }

}
```

Output:

```
a is equal to 10 and b is equal to 20
a is not 0
one variable is equal to the number set in the if
```

In this program we have as many as 3 different conditions within the ifs and starting with the first (&&), we are going to check if two numbers are equal to the preset numbers. If even one of the conditions is not true, then the statements inside the if will not be executed. In the second case (!), on the other hand, we are going to do a negation of the result, that is, the if will execute the block of code only if the condition is not true (in fact a is not equal to 0, however the if is executed). In the third case instead using the || operator, with even only one true condition the if will be executed (even all true or only one).

The Switch statement is useful for having a sort of menu (later we will see how to make an infinite menu that is interrupted by the user) and for having the user choose with input values what our program is going to execute.

This is an example:

```c
#include <stdio.h>

int main()
{
    int a = 0;
    printf("MENU\n");
    printf("insert 0 to print -->Hello World!<--\n");
    printf("insert 1 to print -->Hello<--\n");
    printf("insert 2 to print -->World!<--\n");

    scanf("%d", &a);

    switch(a)
    {
        case 0:
        printf("Hello World!\n");
        break;

        case 1:
        printf("Hello\n");
        break;
```

```
        case 2:
        printf("World!");
        break;
    }

}
```

Output (the input was taken by the keyboard):

```
MENU
insert 0 to print -->Hello World!<--
insert 1 to print -->Hello<--
insert 2 to print -->World!<--
0
Hello World!
```

First several printf's must be put in to let the user understand the choices available, then next a scanf is put in to get an input value. The first thing to note is that the switch has a condition to "observe" in the round brackets, that is, the value of that variable goes to affect which block of code will be executed.

After the case you have to put the value chosen to execute the code (the first case contains 0 and will be executed only if you enter 0).

The break is also important because it stops the program before it messes up variables and prevents it from executing all the code inside the switch.

So far we have seen variables, if, scanf, printf, and they were all more or less easy to "digest" as arguments.

Instead, we are now about to get into the thick of programming, with even more complicated and fun things to create, such as loops, nested loops, arrays, matrices, and other things that will be quite complicated to understand at first, but with a little practice it will all seem clearer to you.

For and While loops

In this chapter, we will discuss For and While loops, which are very useful for going through a number of algorithmic operations and which require many machine cycles to execute.

They can be useful to us, for example, to insert 100 different numbers inside one or more variables, or to check with an Array which numbers are even, which odd, in short they have infinite utility.

First, however, there is a need to make a small introduction to Arrays.

Arrays are "memory cells" that contain data and which we need, for example, to store more than one number or data in general without declaring other superfluous variables.

An Array is two-dimensional and we are going to get the data within the Array through an index (i) which is an integer value.

Some examples of these cycles may be:

```c
#include <stdio.h>

int main()
{
    int i = 0;
    for(i=0;i<10;i++)
    {
        printf("cycle number: %d\n", i);
    }
}
```

The output is (continued on the next page):

```
cycle number: 0
cycle number: 1
cycle number: 2
cycle number: 3
cycle number: 4
cycle number: 5
cycle number: 6
cycle number: 7
cycle number: 8
cycle number: 9
```

Explanation: the for loop executed 10 times the instructions inside the curly brackets, through the condition inserted in the curly brackets (thus in the for).
The first instruction (i = 0;) is the initial condition, i.e., from where our for must start.
The second instruction (i < 10) serves as a "limit" for our for, i.e., a condition that stops the loop.
The third condition is the update condition (i++) which serves to advance the loop and by how much it must advance.

Explained even more easily through the example above, we can say that: i = 0 means that our index (i) must start at the number 0. i < 10 means that the index (i) must reach the number 9 (since if we enter the condition < 10, then i does not reach 10 but 9 and if we want it to reach 10 we have to put <=). By i++ we basically indicate this (i = i + 1) and it means that the for advances one number at a time.

An example of how Arrays can be useful with the for can be this:

```c
#include <stdio.h>

int main()
{
    int i = 0;
    int n = 0;

    printf("insert the dimension of the array: \n");
    scanf("%d", &n);

    int A[n];

    printf("insert %d numbers\n", n);

    for(i=0;i<n;i++)
    {
        scanf("%d", &A[i]);
    }
    for(i=0;i<n;i++)
    {
        printf("you have inserted this numbers: %d\n",
A[i]);
    }

}
```

Output (the input was taken by the keyboard):

```
insert the dimension of the array:
5
insert 5 numbers
```

```
0
1
2
3
4
you have inserted this numbers: 0
you have inserted this numbers: 1
you have inserted this numbers: 2
you have inserted this numbers: 3
you have inserted this numbers: 4
```

In this example there are many things to explain, including the declaration of an array, the size etc.

First we declare 2 variables (integers), including index (i) and size (n is useful to define the size of the array).

The Array is declared to be int A[n] which means "create an integer array of size n" (I will not go into the creation of Arrays now as it will be covered later). In the for we go to enter the condition (i=0;i<n;i++) which means that the for will reach the length of the variable n.

In the curly brackets instead, we insert scanf to take in input n different numbers and change from A[n] to A[i] to scroll the Array according to i (for example, if i is worth 10 and we write A[i], we are attempting to access memory cell number 9 in the Array, because the Array always starts at zero.

In the final for we are going to print all the numbers taken as input so far.

This program is useful for taking very large amounts of numbers (for example, if we have to make a program that takes in input 100 different numbers, without for we would have to make 100 variables with 100 scanf).

Obviously with the for you can also go the "opposite way", i.e. you can iterate an Array from the end towards the beginning.

This is an example:

```
#include <stdio.h>
```

```c
int main()
{
    int i = 0;
    int n = 0;

    printf("insert the dimension of the array: \n");
    scanf("%d", &n);

    int A[n];

    printf("insert %d numbers\n", n);
    for(i=n-1;i>=0;i--)
    {
        scanf("%d", &A[i]);
    }
    for(i=0;i<n;i++)
    {
        printf("you have inserted this numbers: %d\n",
A[i]);
    }

}
```

Output (the input was taken by the keyboard):

```
insert the dimension of the array:
5
insert 5 numbers
0
1
2
3
4
you have inserted this numbers: 4
you have inserted this numbers: 3
you have inserted this numbers: 2
you have inserted this numbers: 1
you have inserted this numbers: 0
```

The for is useful to us when we know the number of times the loop must repeat. But what if we don't know the number of times instead? In this case we can use the while loop, which is very useful to us in cases where we need to stop the loop when a certain condition arises.

This is an example on how to create a while:

```c
#include <stdio.h>
int main()
{
    int i = 0;
    int n = 0;
    while(i==0)
    {
        printf("the values of n is: %d\n", n);
        if(n==9)
        {
            i++;
        }
        n++;
    }

}
```

Output:

```
the value of n is: 0
the value of n is: 1
the value of n is: 2
the value of n is: 3
the value of n is: 4
the value of n is: 5
the value of n is: 6
the value of n is: 7
the value of n is: 8
the value of n is: 9
```

This program will start printing the value of the variable n until it reaches 9, after that through the if stops the while loop. One important thing of course is the condition inside the while (i==0), it means "as long as the variable i is worth 0, then run the code in the curly brackets."

If the condition is false instead then it does not execute anything and exits the loop directly.

If, on the other hand, there is a specific need to execute the loop at least once (even if the condition is false), then we can use do-while, a while-specific condition to execute the code at least once.

Of course, the advantage of the do-while is that it might be useful in somewhat special cases, for example when there is a need to perform a particular check within the program and only proceed later.

One disadvantage, however, is that sometimes the do-while might upset the operation of the program, so it is best if you check before writing if it is necessary.

Here is an example:

```c
#include <stdio.h>

int main()
{
    int i = 0;
    int n = 0;

    do
    {
        printf("the values of n is: %d\n", n);
        if(n==9)
```

```c
        {
            i++;
        }
        n++;

    }while(i==0);

}
```

In this program, the first time the loop will be executed, even if the condition in the while is not true, the statements in the do will be executed once (in the case where the condition is false), while if the condition is true it is a normal while. Nested loops have been referred to several times throughout the previous chapters. However, what exactly are these types of loops and what do they involve? Nested loops are simply loops within other loops and can really consume a lot of execution time and resources.

Here is an example of a nested loop:

```c
#include <stdio.h>

int main()
{
    int i = 0;
    int j = 0;
    int a = 0;

    for(i=0;i<10;i++)
    {
        for(j=0;j<10;j++)
```

```c
        {
            printf("this is a nested loop\n");
        }


    }
}
```

Arrays

Arrays are very useful types of variables that are used to take many different data from each other (e.g. we can take ranges of numbers, characters etc.). Their handling has been covered previously with for and while loops, and in this chapter we are going to dwell on the various types of arrays, how to extract only certain types of data etc.

Just as with variables, Arrays have different types that are useful in different fields, such as a Character Array (useful for use as a string, i.e., a set of characters). Some types can be:

```c
#include <stdio.h>

int main()
{
    int A[10];
    long long int B[10];
    char C[10];
}
```

As mentioned earlier, the number in the square brackets indicates the size of the Array and will start from 0.
An Array can be initialized with values of your choice or you can override them by giving them as input. To initialize the Array this is the syntax:

```c
#include <stdio.h>

int main()
{
    int i = 0;
    int A[10] = {0,1,2,3,4,5,6,7,8,9};
    for(i=0;i<10;i++)
    {
        printf("The Array is: %d\n", A[i]);
    }
}
```

Output:

```
The Array is: 0
The Array is: 1
The Array is: 2
The Array is: 3
The Array is: 4
The Array is: 5
The Array is: 6
The Array is: 7
The Array is: 8
The Array is: 9
```

We can use the char Array to create strings that we can print later.

For example:

```c
#include <stdio.h>

int main()
{
```

```c
    int i = 0;
    char A[12] = {'h','e','l','l','o','
',' W','o','r','l','d','!'};

    printf("The char Array is: \n");

    for(i=0;i<12;i++)
    {
        printf("%c", A[i]);
    }

}
```

Output:

```
The char Array is:
hello World!
```

In this case we initialize the character Array (with Hello World!) and print its characters using the for.

We can also print the string in different ways, such as backwards, from the beginning, starting from the middle etc.
To print it backwards we can do like this:

```c
#include <stdio.h>

int main()
{
    int i = 0;
    char A[12] = {'H','e','l','l','o','
',' W','o','r','l','d','!'};

    printf("The reverse char Array is: \n");
    for(i=12;i>=0;i--)
```

```c
    {
        printf("%c", A[i]);
    }

}
```

Output:

```
The reverse char Array is:
!dlroW olleH
```

We can also use an if to print only chosen characters. Obviously, however, using an if within the for will not actually delete the characters entered in the condition from the Array. In fact, by using this method we are simply not going to print them out, while keeping the Array "intact."

For example:

```c
#include <stdio.h>

int main()
{
    int i = 0;
    char A[12] = {'h','e','l','l','o','
','W','o','r','l','d','!'};

    printf("The char Array is: \n");

    for(i=0;i<12;i++)
    {
        if(A[i]!='l')
        printf("%c", A[i]);
    }

}
```

This code will print all characters within the Array except for the character (l):

```
The char Array is:
heo Word!
```

Multi-dimensional Array

In this chapter, we are going to deal with Multi-dimensional arrays (in this case, two-dimensional arrays). Normal Arrays are one-dimensional, that is, you can only scroll them from left to right and backwards. Two-dimensional Arrays can be, for example, calendars or a Rubik's cube face.

The correct syntax for creating a two-dimensional Array is this:
```
int M[rows][columns]; //number of rows and columns
```

Example:

```
#include <stdio.h>

int main()
{
    int rows = 0;
    int columns = 0;

    printf("enter the number of rows: \n");
    scanf("%d", &rows);

    printf("enter the number of columns: \n");
    scanf("%d", &columns);

    int M[rows][columns];
```

```c
    int i = 0;
    int j = 0;

    printf("insert %d numbers: \n", rows*columns);
    for(i=0;i<rows;i++)
    {
        for(j=0;j<columns;j++)
        {
            scanf("%d", &M[i][j]);
        }
    }

    printf("the two-dimensional Array is: \n");


    for(i=0;i<rows;i++)
    {
        for(j=0;j<columns;j++)
        {
          printf("|%d| ", M[i][j]);
        }
        printf("\n");
    }

}
```

Output (the input was taken from the keyboard):

```
enter the number of rows:
2
enter the number of columns:
2
insert 4 numbers:
0
1
2
3
the two-dimensional Array is:
|0| |1|
|2| |3|
```

An Array of this type that has as its size NxN (that is, the number of rows corresponds to the number of columns) then it is square. The diagonals of the Array are called the "main diagonal" the one that starts from left to right, while the "secondary diagonal" is the one that starts from right to left.

An example on how the main and secondary diagonal can be printed:

```c
#include <stdio.h>
//main diagonal
int main()
{
    int rows = 0;
    int columns = 0;

    printf("enter the number of rows: \n");
    scanf("%d", &rows);

    printf("enter the number of columns: \n");
    scanf("%d", &columns);

    int M[rows][columns];

    int i = 0;
    int j = 0;
    printf("insert %d numbers: \n", rows*columns);
    for(i=0;i<rows;i++)
    {
        for(j=0;j<columns;j++)
        {
            scanf("%d", &M[i][j]);
        }
    }
```

```c
    printf("the main diagonal is: \n");
    for(i=0;i<rows;i++)
    {
        for(j=0;j<columns;j++)
        {
          if(i==j)
          printf("|%d| ", M[i][j]);
          else
          printf("| | ");
        }
        printf("\n");
    }

}
```

An example on how the main and secondary diagonal can be printed:

```c
#include <stdio.h>

//main diagonal

int main()
{
    int rows = 0;
    int columns = 0;

    printf("enter the number of rows: \n");
    scanf("%d", &rows);

    printf("enter the number of columns: \n");
    scanf("%d", &columns);

    int M[rows][columns];
    int i = 0;
    int j = 0;
    printf("insert %d numbers: \n", rows*columns);
    for(i=0;i<rows;i++)
    {
        for(j=0;j<columns;j++)
        {
            scanf("%d", &M[i][j]);
        }
```

```c
        }

    printf("the main diagonal is: \n");
    for(i=0;i<rows;i++)
    {
        for(j=0;j<columns;j++)
        {
          if(i==j)
          printf("|%d| ", M[i][j]);
          else
          printf("| | ");
        }
        printf("\n");
    }
}
```

Output (the input was taken by the keyboard):

```
enter the number of rows:
3
enter the number of columns:
3
insert 9 numbers:
0 1 2 3 4 5 6 7 8
the main diagonal is:
|0| | | | | |
| | |4| | | |
| | | | |8|
```

This is an example to print the secondary diagonal:

```c
#include <stdio.h>

//secondary diagonal

int main()
{
    int rows = 0;
    int columns = 0;

    printf("enter the number of rows: \n");
    scanf("%d", &rows);
```

```c
    printf("enter the number of columns: \n");
    scanf("%d", &columns);

    int M[rows][columns];

    int i = 0;
    int j = 0;

    printf("insert %d numbers: \n", rows*columns);
    for(i=0;i<rows;i++)
    {
        for(j=0;j<columns;j++)
        {
            scanf("%d", &M[i][j]);
        }
    }

    printf("the secondary diagonal is: \n");
    for(i=0;i<rows;i++)
    {
        for(j=0;j<columns;j++)
        {
          if(i+j==(rows-1))
          printf("|%d| ", M[i][j]);
          else
          printf("| | ");
        }
        printf("\n");
    }

}
```

Output (the input was taken by the keyboard):

```
enter the number of rows:
3
enter the number of columns:
3
insert 9 numbers:
0 1 2 3 4 5 6 7 8
the secondary diagonal is:
| | | | |2|
| | |4| | |
```

Obviously, you can create programs to do many kinds of operations with these types of Arrays. An example would be the sum of all rows, columns, diagonals etc.

Here is an example:

```c
#include <stdio.h>

int main()
{
    int rows = 0;
    int columns = 0;
    int sum = 0;

    printf("enter the number of rows: \n");
    scanf("%d", &rows);

    printf("enter the number of columns: \n");
    scanf("%d", &columns);

    int M[rows][columns];

    int i = 0;
    int j = 0;

    printf("insert %d numbers: \n", rows*columns);
    for(i=0;i<rows;i++)
    {
        for(j=0;j<columns;j++)
        {
            scanf("%d", &M[i][j]);
            sum = sum + M[i][j];
        }
```

```c
        printf("the sum (of the %d° rows) is: %d\n", i, sum);
        sum = 0;
    }

}
```

Output (the input was taken by the keyboard):

```
enter the number of rows:
3
enter the number of columns:
3
insert 9 numbers:
0 1 2 3 4 5 6 7 8
the sum (of the 0° rows) is: 3
the sum (of the 1° rows) is: 12
the sum (of the 2° rows) is: 21
```

A vague example on n-dimensional Arrays might be this:

```c
#include <stdio.h>

int main()
{
    int a = 10;
    int b = 10;
    int c = 10;
    int A[a][b][c];

    A[0][0][0] = 0;


}
```

Functions

Functions are powerful tools in the C language. In fact, they save code and reuse it. If we only consider this aspect, functions inherit the concept of procedures or subroutines.

Some languages distinguish between functions that return a value and functions that don't. C assumes that every function returns a value. This is done by using a return statement followed by a value. If we omit the return statement, it does not return a value and cannot be used, for example, on the right-hand side of an assignment or as an argument to another function call.

For example, consider the definition of a function that takes a double and an int, exponentiates it, and returns the result:

```c
#include <stdio.h>

double FunctionPow(double value, int Pow)
{
double return_value = 1.0;
int i;
for(i=0; i<Pow; i++)
{
return_value = return_value * value;
}
return(return_value);
}

int main()
{
    double base_number;
    int Pow;
    double result = 0;
    printf("insert the pow to do: \n");
    scanf("%lf", &base_number);
    scanf("%d", &Pow);
    result = FunctionPow(base_number, Pow);
```

```c
    printf("the result is: %.2lf\n", result);
}
```

Output (the input was taken from the keyboard):

```
insert the pow to do:
2 2
the result is: 4.00
```

The example above is a simple function used to calculate a pow, taking as input the base and exponent. The function is of type double since it may return results with decimals. The values inside the round brackets are the ones to be entered later in the main (the names can be different, in practice the function needs the parameters in the round brackets to be executed). Next we go to assign to the variable "result" the result of the function (which will be executed in that very line of code).
An example of simpler function:

```c
#include <stdio.h>

int sum(int value1, int value2)
{
int result = 0;
result = value1 + value2;
return (result);
}

int main()
{
    int a;
    int b;
    int result = 0;
    printf("insert the number to sum: \n");
    scanf("%d", &a);
    scanf("%d", &b);
    result = sum(a,b);
    printf("the result is: %d\n", result);
}
```

Output (the input was taken from the keyboard):

```
insert the number to sum:
0 2
the result is: 2
```

You can also use boolean variables to create boolean functions that return true if the result is correct (from the if), while returning false if the result is incorrect.

There is an example:

```c
#include <stdio.h>
#include <stdbool.h>

bool BoolFunction(int A)
{
    if(A == 20)
    {
        printf("the result is equal to 20\n");
        return true;
    }
    else printf("the result is not equal to 20\n");

    return false;

}

int main()
{
    int a = 0;
    bool result;
    printf("insert a number: \n");
    scanf("%d", &a);
    result = BoolFunction(a);
    if(result)
    printf("the result is true\n");
    else printf("the result is false\n");
}
```

Output (the input was taken from the keyboard):

```
insert a number:
20
the result is equal to 20
the result is true
```

Structures

Structs are very useful data types for the purpose of creating groupings of different data. For example, this approach is used extensively in **SQL** databases.

The **struct** keyword is used to define the structure in the C language.

The items in the structure are called its member and they can be of any valid data type (int, char etc). To access a given data item within the struct you use dot (.) and you cannot initialize variables within the struct.

Here is an example on structures:

```c
#include <stdio.h>

struct PersonalData
{
    char FirstName[20];
    char LastName[20];
    int age;
    int PhoneNumber;
```

```c
};

int main()
{
    struct PersonalData var1;
    printf("insert the requested data: \n");
    printf("insert the first name: \n");
    scanf("%s", &var1.FirstName);
    printf("insert the last name: \n");
    scanf("%s", &var1.LastName);
    printf("insert the age: \n");
    scanf("%d", &var1.age);
    printf("insert the phone number: \n");
    scanf("%d", &var1.PhoneNumber);
}
```

Output (the input was taken from the keyboard):

```
insert the requested data:
insert the first name:
John
insert the last name:
Brown
insert the age:
20
insert the phone number:
7180123456


the personal data are:
FirstName-->John<-- LastName-->Brown<--
age-->20<-- PhoneNumber-->7180123456<--
```

The above code might give you warnings, since to print the Character Arrays I used the %s which would be the specific format of strings. It depends on which compiler you use.

Here is another example of using structs to take different values:

```c
#include <stdio.h>

struct PersonalData
{
    int age;
};

int main()
{
    struct PersonalData var1;
    struct PersonalData var2;
    printf("insert the first data (age): \n");
    scanf("%d", &var1.age);
    printf("insert the second data (age): \n");
    scanf("%d", &var2.age);
    printf("the first data is: %d, the second data is: %d", var1.age, var2.age);
}
```

Output (the input was taken from the keyboard):

```
insert the first data (age):
20
insert the second data (age):
30
the first data is: 20, the second data is: 30
```

In this specific case and with this code, we are going to create two different struct variables (var1 and var2) by having the struct remain unchanged and changing the values by storing them in the two previously created variables.

If you try to initialize variables within structs, the compiler will give an error:

```c
#include <stdio.h>


struct PersonalData
{
    int age = 0;// you can't initialize it in the struct
};
```

```c
int main()
{
    struct PersonalData var1;
    struct PersonalData var2;

    printf("insert the first data (age): \n");
    scanf("%d", &var1.age);

    printf("insert the second data (age): \n");
    scanf("%d", &var2.age);

    printf("the first data is: %d, the second data is:
%d", var1.age, var2.age);
}
```

In this case the code is wrong.

Stack and queue

The term stack denotes a list of variable length in which both data entries and extractions occur only at one end. Consequently, in a stack the first extractable element is the one that was inserted last: it is called the surfacing element, and the method by which a computer accesses a stack of data is called the L.I.F.O. method, which stands for Last In First Out.

In computer science, we use the term queue to denote a list of variable length, in which all insertions are made after the last element (called the bottom of the queue) while all extractions with possible elimination occur on the first element (called the head of the queue). This means that the first element that can be extracted is the one that was inserted first-that is why we talk about the F.I.F.O. method, which stands for First In First Out.

The basic operations of the stack are:
Push: adds an element to the top.
Pop: removes the top element.
Show: print all the element.

Here is an example without code of a stack:
Push("0");
Push("1");
Push("2");
Pop(); //2
Pop(); //1
Pop(); //0

With this order in the stack there are the following items (sorted): 2, 1, 0 (Last In First Out, so the number 2 is the first to print).

Here is an example of a program with the stack:

```c
#include <stdio.h>
#include <stdlib.h>

#define size 10

int top = -1;
int stack[size];

void push()
{
    int a;
    if (top == size - 1)
    {
        printf("too much elements\n");
    }

    else

    {
        printf("enter the element to be added onto the stack: \n");
        scanf("%d", &a);
        top = top + 1;
        stack[top] = a;
```

```c
    }
}


void pop()
{
    if (top == -1)
    {
        printf("there    are    no    elements    to    pop
(extract)\n");
    }
    else
    {
        printf("extracted element: %d\n", stack[top]);
        top = top - 1;
    }
}


void show()
{
    int i;

    if (top == -1)
    {
        printf("there are no elements to print\n");
    }

    else
    {
        printf("elements present in the stack: \n");
        for (i=top;i>=0;i--)
            printf("%d\n", stack[i]);
    }

}
```

```c
int main()
{
    printf("operations on the stack: \n");

    printf("1.push        the        element\n2.pop        the
element\n3.show\n4.end\n");

    int choice;

    while (1)
    {
        printf("enter the choice: \n");
        scanf("%d", &choice);
        switch (choice)
        {
        case 1:
            push();
            break;

        case 2:
            pop();
            break;

        case 3:
            show();
            break;

        case 4:
            exit(0);

        default:
            printf("\nmake another choice\n");
        }
    }
}
```

Output (the input was taken from the keyboard):

```
operations on the stack:
1.push the element
2.pop the element
```

```
3.show
4.end
enter the choice:
1
enter the element to be added onto the stack:
10
enter the choice:
1
enter the element to be added onto the stack:
20
enter the choice:
3
elements present in the stack:
20
10
enter the choice:
4
```

The first thing to do for the stack is to declare two libraries (the usual one plus another one that is used for the exit function). Then we define the size of the stack with a static value and write the three functions that can be useful to us. Let us go to analyze the first function (push): with an if we go to check the size of the top variable and if it reaches the size of the stack minus 1, then it means that the stack is full. This function is used to add elements within the stack. The function (pop) is used to extract (and remove) elements within the stack. In the if we go to check if the top variable is minus 1, then it means the stack is empty, otherwise it extracts the element and reduces the top index. With the (show) function, the principle is the same as with the (pop) function, only instead of extracting and deleting, elements are printed and not removed.

Now we will look at the queue, which has a similar approach to the stack but of the First In First Out type, that is, the first element in is the first element out.

There is an example of queue (the theory has already been explained):

```c
#include <stdio.h>
#include <stdlib.h>
#define size 10

int queue[size];
int end = - 1;
int front = - 1;

void insert()
{
    int InsertItem;
    if(end == size - 1)
       printf("too many elements in the queue \n");
    else
    {
        if(front == - 1)
        front = 0;

        printf("insert the element in the queue\n : ");
        scanf("%d", &InsertItem);
        end = end + 1;
        queue[end] = InsertItem;
    }
}

void delete()
{
    if(front == - 1 || front > end)
    {
        printf("there are no items to eliminate \n");
        return ;
    }

    else
```

```c
    {
        printf("element deleted from the queue: %d\n",
queue[front]);
        front = front + 1;
    }
}

void show()
{
    int i;
    if(front == - 1)
        printf("the queue is empty \n");
    else
    {
        printf("the queue is: \n");
        for (i=front;i<=end;i++)
            printf("%d ", queue[i]);
        printf("\n");
    }
}

int main()
{
    int choice;
    printf("1.insert operation\n");
    printf("2.delete operation\n");
    printf("3.print the queue\n");
    printf("4.exit\n");
    while (1)
    {
        printf("enter your choice of operations: ");
        scanf("%d", &choice);
        switch(choice)
        {

            case 1:
            insert();
            break;

            case 2:
            delete();
            break;
```

```c
              case 3:
              show();
              break;
              case 4:
              exit(0);

              default:
              printf("make another choice \n");
          }
      }
}
```

Output (the input was taken from the keyboard):

```
1.insert operation
2.delete operation
3.print the queue
4.exit
enter your choice of operations: 1
insert the element in the queue: 10
enter your choice of operations: 1
insert the element in the queue: 20
enter your choice of operations: 3
the queue is:
10 20
enter your choice of operations: 2
element deleted from the queue: 10
enter your choice of operations: 2
element deleted from the queue: 20
enter your choice of operations: 4
```

The code to write for the queue is similar to the code already written for the stack, except that you must have a First In First Out approach. We use the two libraries, create the queue with the necessary variables and define the size. Then we write the functions to insert, extract (and delete) and print. In the function (insert), if end reaches the size minus 1, then it means the queue is full, otherwise it adds elements. The function (delete) is for deleting elements and it checks if there are no elements then it prints that no elements can be deleted. The function (show) is simply to print the elements and does not delete them from the queue.

In the next chapter we are going to address another important feature of C, which is reading and writing from a file (such as a text file, .txt).

Reading and writing from a file

In the C language it is possible to read and write to many types of files (usually the .txt text file is used). In this chapter we are going to use a type of object not covered so far, namely pointers. A pointer is a variable that holds the memory address of another variable. It allows us both to work "low-level" (with physical machine addresses) and to abstract complex data structures, all while maintaining some simplicity. In this case we need a pointer of type FILE and we use the pointer fp:

```c
FILE *fp;
```

The main function are:

```c
fopen(): creates a new file or opens an existing file
fclose(): closes a file
fscanf(): reads a set of data from a file
fprintf(): writes a set of data to a file
```

Operators to handle a file:

```c
r: open a file in read mode
w: opens or creates a text file in write mode
a: opens a file in add mode
r+: opens a file in both read and write mode
a+: opens a file in both read and write mode
w+: opens a file in both read and write mode
```

This is an example of a program that opens the file, writes something (integers), and closes the file:

```c
#include <stdio.h>

int main()
{
    FILE *fp;
    int n;
    int data;
    int i;

    fp = fopen("hello.txt", "w");
    if (fp == NULL) {
        printf("file opening error\n");
        return 1;
    }

    printf("how much data do you want to enter?\n");
    scanf("%d", &n);
```

```c
    printf("insert %d data:\n", n);

    for (i=0;i<n;i++)
    {
        scanf("%d", &data);
        fprintf(fp, "%d ", data);
    }


    fclose(fp);
}
```

Output (the input was taken from the keyboard):

```
how much data do you want to enter?
5
insert 5 data:
0 1 2 3 4
```

On the file is writed:
```
0 1 2 3 4
```

If instead you want a program that reads from the file and prints, you can write it like this example:

```c
#include <stdio.h>

int main()
{
    FILE *fp;
    int data;
    int i;

    fp = fopen("hello.txt", "r");
    if (fp == NULL) {
        printf("file opening error\n");
        return 1;
    }


    printf("data on the file: \n");
    while (fscanf(fp, "%d", &data) == 1) {
```

```c
        printf("%d ", data);
    }

    fclose(fp);
}
```

Output (the input was taken from the keyboard):

```
data on the file:
0 1 2 3 4
```

In the next chapter, there will be exercises, possible solutions and challenges to practice all the topics covered so far.

Exercises and possible solutions

Exercise:

0: Given two numbers as input print as output their average. Example: a = 20, b = 10, average = 15.

1: Given as input the side of a square print as output its perimeter and area.

Example: side = 10, perimeter = 40, area = 100.

2: Given an integer as input, print as output its square and cube.

Example: input = 2, square = 4, cube = 8.

3: Write a program that takes as input 3 numbers determine whether they can be considered in arithmetic progression; an arithmetic progression is a series of numbers in which the difference between two successive numbers is constant.
Example: the progression could be 15, 10, 5, because 15-10 = 5, 10-5 = 5.

4: Given as input a 5-digit number print as output the sum of the digits of the number.

5: Given as input a value from 1 to 10, print as output its table.

6: Write a program that outputs all numbers less than 2000 and that divided by 24, 30 or 18 gives the remainder 7.

7: A perfect number is perfect if the number is equal to the sum of its divisors. Given as input a number n, print as output whether n is perfect or not. (Example: N=28 is perfect because 28=1+2+4+7+14)

8: Write a program that finds the maximum number between two numbers taken as input and prints them out.

9: Write a program that takes as input a year and tells whether it is leap year or not. A year is a leap year if it is:
(a) divisible by 4 and **NOT** divisible by 100.
(b) divisible by 400.

10: Write a program that takes as input a number n and calculates the following expression: $(3n-2)^{\wedge}2$.

11: Write a program that outputs all two-digit numbers that divided by 15 give remainder equal to the square of the quotient. Example: such a number is 34 because 34:15 = 2 remainder 4 and 2^2=4.

12: Output all 3-digit numbers that have the digits in ascending order and their sum equals 18. Example: A possible number is 279.

13: Write a program that asks for N numbers as input and then prints out the first N numbers of the Fibonacci succession. Recall that the Fibonacci succession is a sequence of positive integers in which each number beginning with the third is the sum of the previous two. For example if N=9 we will have the following terms 1 , 1 , 2 , 3 , 5 , 8 , 13 , 21 , 34.

14: Write a program that takes as input an integer representing a time in minutes and transforms it into hours, minutes, seconds.

15: Write a program that enters N numbers from the keyboard and counts the positive and negative ones.

16: Write a function that receives as parameters two integers a and b (b > -1) and returns the result of the power a^b.

17: Write a program containing a function that is used to print out multiplication tables from 1 to 10.

18: Write a program that prints a choice menu with the switch-case.

19: Write a program using the two-dimensional Array (matrix) that sum all the columns.

20: Write a program that reads data from a text file (.txt extension) and encrypts it using Caesar's cipher. Caesar's cipher works like this: each letter is moved 5 positions forward in the alphabet. For example, if we have the letter "a" it will become "f", the letter "b" will become "g" etc. It then creates another file (.txt) that contains the cipher text.

Possible solutions:

Exercise 0:

```c
#include <stdio.h>

int main()
{
    int a, b;
    float average;

    //read the two numbers as input
    printf("enter the first number: ");
    scanf("%d", &a);

    printf("enter the second number: ");
    scanf("%d", &b);

    //calculate the average
    average = (a + b) / 2.0;

    //print the average as output
```

```c
    printf("the average is: %.2f\n", average);

}
```

Exercise 1:

```c
#include <stdio.h>

int main()
{
    float side;
    float SquarePerimeter = 0;
    float SquareArea = 0;

    printf("insert the side of the square: ");
    scanf("%f", &side);


    SquarePerimeter = side*4;
    SquareArea = side*side;

    printf("the perimeter of the square is: %.2f\n",
SquarePerimeter);
    printf("the area of the square is: %.2f",
SquareArea);

}
```

Exercise 2:

```c
#include <stdio.h>

int main()
{
    int num;
    int square, cube;

    // Read the integer as input
    printf("enter an integer: ");
```

```c
    scanf("%d", &num);

    // Calculate the square and cube
    square = num*num;

    cube = num*num*num;

    // Print the square and cube as output
    printf("square: %d\n", square);

    printf("cube: %d\n", cube);

}
```

Exercise 3:

```c
#include <stdio.h>

int main() {
    int num1, num2, num3;

    printf("Enter the first number: ");
    scanf("%d", &num1);
    printf("Enter the second number: ");
    scanf("%d", &num2);
    printf("Enter the third number: ");
    scanf("%d", &num3);

    if (num2 - num1 == num3 - num2) {

        printf("The numbers form an arithmetic
progression.\n");

    } else {
        printf("The numbers do not form an arithmetic
progression.\n");
    }

}
```

Exercise 4:

```c
#include <stdio.h>

int main()
{
    int number;
    int sum = 0;
    int digit;

    printf("enter a 5-digit number: ");
    scanf("%d", &number);

    while (number > 0) {
        int digit = number % 10;
        sum = sum + digit;
        number = number / 10;
    }

    printf("sum of the digits: %d\n", sum);
}
```

Exercise 5:

```c
#include <stdio.h>

int main()
{
    int number;
    int i;

    printf("enter a number from 1 to 10: ");
    scanf("%d", &number);

    if(number < 1 || number > 10) {

        printf("please enter a number from 1 to 10.\n");
        return 1;

    }

    //print the multiplication table of the given number

    printf("multiplication table of %d:\n", number);
```

```c
    for (i=1;i<=10;i++) {

        printf("%d x %d = %d\n", number, i, number * i);

    }

}
```

Exercise 6:

```c
#include <stdio.h>

int main() {
    int limit = 2000;
    int remainder = 7;
    int num;

    for (num=0;num<limit;num++) {

        if (num % 24 == remainder || num % 30 ==
remainder || num % 18 == remainder) {
            printf("%d\n", num);
        }

    }

}
```

Exercise 7:

```c
#include <stdio.h>

int main()
{
    int n;
    int sum = 0;
    int i;
```

```c
    printf("enter a number: ");
    scanf("%d", &n);

    for (i=1;i<=n/2;i++) {
        if (n % i == 0) {
            sum += i;
        }
    }

    //check if the number is perfect
    if (sum == n) {

        printf("%d is a perfect number\n", n);

    } else {

        printf("%d is not a perfect number\n", n);

    }
}
```

Exercise 8:

```c
#include <stdio.h>

int main() {
    int num1;
    int num2;

    printf("enter the first number: ");
    scanf("%d", &num1);

    printf("enter the second number: ");
    scanf("%d", &num2);

    if(num1>num2) {
        printf("the maximum number is: %d\n", num1);
    } else {
        printf("the maximum number is: %d\n", num2);
    }

}
```

Exercise 9:

```c
#include <stdio.h>

int main() {
    int year;

    printf("enter a year: ");
    scanf("%d", &year);

    if((year%4==0&&year%100!=0)||year%400==0) {
        printf("%d is a leap year.\n", year);
    } else {
        printf("%d is not a leap year.\n", year);
    }

}
```

Exercise 10:

```c
#include <stdio.h>

int main() {
    int n;
    int result;

    printf("enter a number (n): ");
    scanf("%d", &n);

    result = (3 * n - 2) * (3 * n - 2);

    printf("(3 * %d - 2)^2 = %d\n", n, result);

}
```

Exercise 11:

```c
#include <stdio.h>

int main()
{
    int num;
    int quotient;
    int remainder;

    printf("two-digit numbers that divided by 15 give
remainder equal to the square of the quotient:\n");

    for (num = 10; num <= 99; num++) {
        quotient = num / 15;
        remainder = num % 15;
        if (remainder == (quotient * quotient)) {
            printf("%d\n", num);
        }
    }

}
```

Exercise 12:

```c
#include <stdio.h>

int main() {

    int num;
    int digit1;
    int digit2;
    int digit3;

    printf("3-digit numbers with digits in ascending
order and sum equal to 18:\n");

    for(num=102;num<=987;num++) {

        digit1 = num / 100;
        digit2 = (num / 10) % 10;
        digit3 = num % 10;
```

```c
        if(digit1<digit2 && digit2<digit3 &&
(digit1+digit2+digit3) == 18) {

            printf("%d\n", num);

        }
    }

}
```

Exercise 13:

```c
#include <stdio.h>

int main()
{
    int N;
    int i;
    printf("enter the value of N: ");
    scanf("%d", &N);

    if(N <= 0)
    {
        printf("N must be a positive integer.\n");
        return 0;
    }

    int fibonacci[N];

    fibonacci[0] = 1;//the first two numbers are 1

    fibonacci[1] = 1;

    for(i = 2; i < N; i++)
    {
        fibonacci[i] = fibonacci[i - 1] + fibonacci[i -
2];
    }
```

```c
    printf("the first %d numbers of the Fibonacci
sequence are:\n", N);
    for(i = 0; i < N; i++)
    {
        printf("%d ", fibonacci[i]);
    }

}
```

Exercise 14:

```c
#include <stdio.h>

int main()
{
    int TotalMinutes, hours, minutes, seconds;

    printf("enter the time in minutes: ");
    scanf("%d", &TotalMinutes);

    if(TotalMinutes < 0)
    {
        printf("time cannot be negative.\n");
        return 0;
    }

    hours = TotalMinutes / 60;        // Extract hours
    minutes = TotalMinutes % 60;      // Extract remaining
minutes
    seconds = minutes * 60;           // Convert remaining
minutes to seconds

    printf("time in hours %d\nminutes %d\nseconds %d\n ",
hours, minutes, seconds);

}
```

Exercise 15:

```c
#include <stdio.h>

int main()
{
    int N;
    int i;
    int number;

    int positiveCount = 0;
    int negativeCount = 0;

    printf("enter the value of N: ");
    scanf("%d", &N);

    if(N <= 0)
    {
        printf("N must be a positive integer\n");
        return 0;
    }

    printf("enter %d numbers:\n", N);

    for(i = 0; i < N; i++)
    {
        scanf("%d", &number);

        if(number > 0)
        {
            positiveCount++;
        }

        if(number < 0)
        {
            negativeCount++;
        }
    }

    printf("positive numbers: %d\n", positiveCount);

    printf("negative numbers: %d\n", negativeCount);

}
```

Exercise 16:

```c
#include <stdio.h>

long long int power(int a, int b) {

    if (b < 0) {

        printf("error: b must be greater than or equal to
0.\n");
        return -1;

    }

    long long int result = 1;


    while (b > 0)
    {
        if (b % 2 == 1) {
            result *= a;
        }

        a *= a;
        b /= 2;
    }

    return result;
}

int main()
{
    int a, b;
    printf("enter the value of a: ");
    scanf("%d", &a);

    printf("enter the value of b (b > -1): ");
    scanf("%d", &b);
```

```c
    long long int result = power(a, b);

    if (result != -1) {
        printf("%d ^ %d = %lld\n", a, b, result);
    }

}
```

Exercise 17:

```c
#include <stdio.h>

void MultiplicationTable(int num)
{
    int i;
    printf("multiplication table for %d:\n", num);
    for (i = 1; i <= 10; i++)
    {
        printf("%d x %d = %d\n", num, i, num * i);
    }
    printf("\n");
}

int main()
{
    int i;
    for (i = 1; i <= 10; i++)
    {
        MultiplicationTable(i);
    }
}
```

Exercise 18:

```c
#include <stdio.h>

int main() {
    int choice;

    do {
        printf("-->Choice Menu<--\n");
        printf("option 1\n");
        printf("option 2\n");
        printf("option 3\n");
        printf("exit\n");
        printf("enter your choice (1-4): ");
        scanf("%d", &choice);

        switch (choice) {
            case 1:
                printf("you have selected option 1\n");
                break;
            case 2:
                printf("you have selected option 2\n");
                break;
            case 3:
                printf("you have selected option 3\n");
                break;
            case 4:
                printf("exiting the program\n");
                break;
            default:
                printf("please choose another option\n");
                break;
        }

        printf("\n");
    }while(choice != 4);

}
```

Exercise 19:

```c
#include <stdio.h>
```

```c
int main()
{
    int rows;
    int columns;
    int i;
    int j;

    printf("enter the number of rows: ");
    scanf("%d", &rows);

    printf("enter the number of columns: ");
    scanf("%d", &columns);

    int matrix[rows][columns];

    printf("enter the elements of the matrix:\n");

    for (i = 0; i < rows; i++) {

        for (j = 0; j < columns; j++) {

            scanf("%d", &matrix[i][j]);

        }

    }

    int columnSum[columns];
    for (j = 0; j < columns; j++) {

        columnSum[j] = 0;

    }

    for (i = 0; i < rows; i++) {

        for (j = 0; j < columns; j++) {

            columnSum[j] += matrix[i][j];

        }
```

```c
    }

    printf("\ntwo dimensional Array:\n");
    for (i = 0; i < rows; i++) {
        for (j = 0; j < columns; j++) {
            printf("%d ", matrix[i][j]);
        }
        printf("\n");
    }

    printf("\ncolumn sum:\n");
    for (j = 0; j < columns; j++) {
        printf("column %d: %d\n", j, columnSum[j]);
    }

}
```

Exercise 20:

```c
#include <stdio.h>

void encryptText(char* input, char* output, int shift)
    {
    FILE* inputFile = fopen(input, "r");
    FILE* outputFile = fopen(output, "w");

    if (inputFile == NULL || outputFile == NULL) {

        printf("error opening files\n");
        return 1;

    }

    char ch;

    while ((ch = fgetc(inputFile)) != EOF)
    {//EOF stands for End Of File

        //check if the character is a letter
```

```c
        if ('A' <= ch && ch <= 'Z') {

            ch = ((ch - 'A') + shift) % 26 + 'A';

        } else if ('a' <= ch && ch <= 'z') {

            ch = ((ch - 'a') + shift) % 26 + 'a';

        }

        fputc(ch, outputFile);
    }

    fclose(inputFile);
    fclose(outputFile);
}

int main()
{
    char inputFileName[100];
    char outputFileName[100];

    printf("enter the name of the input file (with .txt
extension and you have to create the file): ");
    scanf("%s", inputFileName);

    printf("enter the name of the output file (with .txt
extension): ");
    scanf("%s", outputFileName);

    //call the function
    encryptText(inputFileName, outputFileName, 5);

    printf("encryption complete\n");
}
```

Tricks and tips

In this chapter, we are going to cover many tricks and tips of programming in c. Some deal with how to save compile or run time, others with how to save lines of code. Still others will deal with libraries or pieces of code for algorithms or other useful things.

Tips 0:
To quickly increment a variable by one unit just write i++ (if we write i = i+1 it is the same thing). You can also do it the other way around by using ++i. The main difference is: These are post-increment and pre-increment. In the former case (i++) the variable is incremented after the operation has been executed; in the latter case (++i) the variable is incremented before the operation is executed.
For example, if we have two such instructions:

```
i = 0;
a = i++; // a is 0 and i is 1

i = 0;
a = ++i; // both a and i are 1
```

Tips 1:

In the for loops for example, you may not even have created the index variable i and you can create it directly in the for. If you used the syntax for(i=0;i<n;i++) before, you had to create the variable i previously. Instead, to create it in the for just do for(int i=0;i<n;i++). Be careful, though, because the variable created this way is not recognized outside that loop, because if you try to use it outside, the compiler will return an error.

Tips 2:
Variables can be created mainly in two ways. You can create them in the main, or even before the main, such as under libraries. By creating it this way, the variable is called "global," so doing so it can be used in all functions, in the main, etc. This type of variable, since it can be updated wherever you want, is useful in some cases and will have incorrect values in others. So be careful when creating this type of variable.

Tips 3:
Some times, unfortunately, debugging does not work. For those who don't know what debugging is, it is a useful practice to eliminate errors within code; with complicated programs it doesn't really work well. So this advice may seem obvious to you at first, but you have to use the printf function. If the program doesn't work and you can't pinpoint the problem, use lots of printf to determine which section of code works and which doesn't. For example, if you are sure that a loop is not working, use a printf before and after the execution of that loop, so you can figure out where the problem is.

Tips 4:

Dynamic memory allocation: In C, you can allocate memory dynamically at runtime using functions like malloc, calloc, and realloc. These functions allow you to request memory from the heap.

malloc(): Allocates a block of memory of the given size and returns a pointer to the first byte of the block.
calloc(): Allocates memory for an array of elements and initializes them to zero.
realloc(): Resizes a previously allocated memory block. It can be used to increase or decrease the size of the block.
Freeing allocated memory: Whenever you allocate memory using the dynamic memory allocation functions, it's important to free that memory when you're done using it.

free(): Deallocates the memory previously allocated by malloc, calloc, or realloc.
Avoiding memory leaks: To prevent memory leaks, always pair each call to memory allocation functions with a corresponding call to free when you're finished using the allocated memory. It's a good practice to free memory before losing access to the pointer, ensuring that you don't orphan memory.

Buffer overflows and underflows: Improper memory access can lead to buffer overflows (writing beyond allocated memory) or buffer underflows (reading before allocated memory). These issues can result in program crashes or security vulnerabilities. Be cautious when using arrays and pointers to access memory.
Always initialize pointers to **NULL** to avoid using uninitialized pointers.
Use sizeof operator to allocate the right amount of memory, especially when dealing with arrays or structures.
Check the return value of memory allocation functions to handle allocation failures gracefully.
Be cautious when reallocating memory, as it may involve copying data, which can be inefficient.

Remember, proper memory management is essential for writing stable and reliable C programs. Debugging memory-related issues can be challenging, so practicing good memory management habits from the start can save you a lot of time.

Tips 5:
If you use characters, on some compilers you may face an error with scanf("%c), because if there are 2 consecutive scanf() with reading for characters, the program will not work correctly. This happens because when the scanf() function takes the first character, it also includes the sequence \n which means carriage return, the second scanf() then will not work as it should.

This is an example of this error:

```c
#include <stdio.h>

int main()
{
    char a;
    char b;
    printf("insert 2 characters: \n");
    scanf("%c", &a);
    printf("a is: %c\n", a);
    scanf("%c", &b);
    printf("b is: %c\n", b);
}
```

Output (the input was taken from the keyboard):

```
insert 2 characters:
a
```

```
a is: a
b is:
```

In this case, we can enter only one initial character, and the program will skip the second scanf(). If we enter all inputs in the initial line (without pressing enter) then it will work. But there is an easier way to make it work, which is to write scanf(" %c") instead of scanf("%c"). The space difference between the percent and the quotation marks will allow you to enter the characters normally.

Tips 6:
To optimize your C code using compiler flags (or pragmas), you need to pass the appropriate optimization flags to the compiler during the compilation process. Different compilers have different flags for optimization.

Optimization levels:
GCC provides different optimization levels that you can specify using the -O flag, followed by a level number (0, 1, 2, 3, or s for size optimization):
-O0: No optimization (default).
-O1: Basic optimization.
-O2: More aggressive optimization.
-O3: High level of optimization.
-Os: Optimize for size.

Target Architecture:
You can specify the target architecture for better optimization using the –march=ARCHITECTURE and -mtune flags. These flags help the compiler generate instructions optimized for your specific CPU architecture. Replace ARCHITECTURE with the appropriate architecture name (nehalem, skylake) etc.

Aggressive Optimizations:

Be cautious when using these flags, as they can sometimes lead to unexpected behavior.
Remember that compiler optimization can sometimes result in code that behaves differently or is harder to debug.

Example:

```c
#include <stdio.h>
#pragma GCC optimize ("-01")
int main()
{
    //code
}
```

Tips 7:
In this there are 2, namely: \n and \t are useful characters for carriage return and tabbing with printf. In the second tip, however, it is about arithmetic operations. In some cases (especially with older compilers) it is necessary to specify that variables should have value 0. In fact, if we go to create a variable and sum it with a number, the sum may be wrong precisely because the variable is not initialized. Since variables are essentially pointers, then they take the value of the memory cell, which are pseudo-random numbers.

Tips 8:
If you need a function that randomly generates numbers from a "seed," you can use this:

```c
#include <stdio.h>
#include <stdlib.h>
#include <time.h>

int main() {
    srand(time(NULL));
    int RandomNum;
    for (int i = 0; i < 8; i++) {
        RandomNum = rand();
```

```c
        printf("random Number %d: %d\n", i, RandomNum);
    }
}
```

In this case the "seed" used is the current time on the present on the computer, and note well that the results depend precisely on the time, and thus are pseudo-random.

The guide ends here. We have seen a general and basic introduction to the C language, which has made the history of programming languages and is still useful for getting introduced to this topic. Special and due thanks are due to you dear readers, who chose to buy this guide.